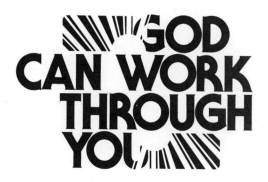

GOD CAN WORK THROUGH YOU

B. Otto Wheeley

Judson Press® Valley Forge

GOD CAN WORK THROUGH YOU

Versions of the Bible quoted in this volume are:

The Holy Bible, King James Version.

The Revised Standard Version of the Bible, copyrighted 1952 and 1971 by the Division of Christian Education of the National Council of the Churches of Christ in the United States of America. Used by permission.

The Living Bible. Copyright 1971 by Tyndale House Publishers, Wheaton, Illinois.

Library of Congress Cataloging in Publication Data

Wheeley, B. Otto
  God can work through you.

  1. Christian life—1960-   2. Witness bearing
(Christianity) I. Title.
BV4501.2.W439   248'.4   77-1130
ISBN 0-8170-0739-3

Dedicated to my wife, Kathleen, whose love, encouragement, and help have made a great difference in what has been done in my life with the gifts God gave me.

PREFACE

If a group of twelve apostles in the first century could be so effective in spreading the gospel of Jesus Christ that the results, referred to in their day as "turning the world upside down," could continue to have some effect on the world twenty centuries later, what in the world is wrong with us Christians today that, collectively, we scarcely create a ripple in our individual local communities? Could it be, as someone has aptly put it, that we of the church are *over*committeed and *under*committed? Could it be that we are so busy with "programs" and telling vast numbers of people in all walks of life how to run their businesses that we are failing to influence and change individual lives? I *am not* against organization, program, or committees *until* they absorb so much time that the individual Christian has no time or commitment to a personal devotional life and ministry through the local church and the work of Christ.

The church must first succeed in the spiritual development of people if the church or other institutions are to succeed in the social or economic development of people. The church is the only institution that even pretends to deal with the spiritual aspect of people; therefore, we must not let it fail in its mission.

There is ample evidence to suggest that individual churches and individual people committed to serving God can and do make a difference and have done so throughout recorded history.

There are individual churches in many denominations that are dealing with the spiritual needs of people and are growing. Some of these have been documented by Elmer L. Towns in his book *Ten Largest Sunday Schools and What Makes Them Grow.* Strong similarities among these churches are emphasis on home visitation, Bible study, and a committed and able leader or leaders.

As we look back into history and the Bible, we can find many individuals who made a major difference to their community, country, or cause. Examples in history are Winston Churchill to England and all of Europe; Joan of Arc to France; Martin Luther to the church and European history. In the Bible outstanding examples of one person making a difference are Abraham, Joseph, Noah, Moses, Gideon, and Paul.

The purpose of this book is to share some thoughts and experiences that may help some readers to know they can make a difference or may help readers to help others to want to make a difference in this world—a difference that will make the world better for all.

Let's try it—then maybe we'll have more need for organization and program, too! In addition, perhaps, as Christians we will move toward fulfilling Christ's command that we must be perfect, as our heavenly Father is perfect (Matthew 5:48).

INTRODUCTION

I have known Otto Wheeley as a committed Christian layman, Bible teacher, corporate executive, civic leader, author, and devoted family man.

With deep Christian commitment to the Lord and His work, his witness has been felt and appreciated by his family, his church, business, government, civic, and academic associates around the world. In going from chemical engineer to senior vice-president of the Koppers Company, he has consistently addressed himself to serving his fellowman.

He has consistently and generously shared his interest, time, thought, and actions with the problems and opportunities of his church, its denomination, institutions of higher learning, and the community in which he lives.

Corporations, institutions, and groups, large and small, recognize and feel his positive influence and leadership. Representative reminders include: the Koppers Company, American Baptist Churches of Pennsylvania and Delaware, The University of Tennessee, the Rankin Christian Center, The Tri-Boro Housing Corporation, marketing fraternities, Blue Cross of Western Pennsylvania, and Alderson-Broaddus

College. But paramount to him is his love for our Lord and dedication to His use of his talents in all situations.

In turn, his service and leadership have been recognized by these organizations—as a senior officer of his company—as an outstanding engineering graduate—and as Marketing Man of the Year—Layman of the Year—and an honorary doctorate degree.

Mr. Wheeley is an example of what this book is all about— one person indeed can make a difference--you and I can make a difference.

Otis Bowden II
President
Bowden & Company, Inc.

CONTENTS

Would You Do It Again?

CHAPTER 1

We introduced ourselves, my wife and I, as being from the local Baptist church and asked if we could come in. Eric hesitatingly responded, "Please do." Mutual friends had suggested that we call because Eric had responded to their invitation to attend church with questions they could not answer. His wife had evidenced interest in attending both Bible study and worship but wanted the entire family to start together. They had been living in the community three or four years, were about thirty years in age, and had lived on occasion in different parts of the country.

I quickly explained who had suggested that we call and that our purpose was to invite the entire family to our church for Bible study and worship on Sunday morning. Eric's wife, Betty, was out for the evening; but their two-year-old daughter was home and very much awake.

Eric, too, was quick to come to the point. He said that he had attended Sunday school as a child but had gotten little out of it. Since becoming an adult, he had sensed a need for more out of life and had tried several churches but always came away empty. His reluctant conclusion had been that "the church was an opiate to salve peoples' feelings so t]   they might feel better." He didn't see people acting any diff   ntly in their daily lives; he also thought that different people had different gods they worshiped and that one god was probably as good as another as long as the person felt better.

I acknowledged the truth of the multiplicity of "gods" abounding in society, but said that my purpose was to talk about the one true God, the God of creation mentioned in the Bible, who loved us so much that he came to earth in fleshly form as Jesus Christ, lived and suffered, was tempted as we, and was crucified—all as part of a plan to reconcile us to himself that, through faith and trust, we might have life and have it more abundantly now and eternally with him. This I knew from my own experience, I said.

At this point Eric responded by saying, "You are an officer in a big corporation. You must be able and intelligent, or you wouldn't be in that position." He continued: "I'm a college graduate, professionally trained, and I think reasonably intelligent. [He was an engineer.] You obviously are sincere in your belief; so you should be able to prove to me there is a God like you say. Prove it to me, and I'll come to Bible study and church, too."

Eric remained courteous and firm, but his interest seemed to be picking up as he anticipated either my "proof" or a hasty retreat. We were in very direct eye contact now. He gently admonished his young daughter to be quieter while her daddy was busy in conversation, and my wife quietly took over holding her attention so that my dialogue with Eric would not be interrupted at this critical point. My response was very deliberate and along the following lines, which I felt God had led me to use under similar circumstances before.

"Eric, I can't prove to you that God exists; but with your permission I believe it will be possible within a few minutes' time and with God's help to respond satisfactorily to your question, which I accept as a sincere inquiry on your part."

He assured me of his sincerity and urged me to go ahead.

I continued, "Please hear my whole answer, Eric; then we'll discuss it further as you may wish.

"First," I said, "you don't really want proof of everything about God, because if you could fully prove God in that sense, you would be equal to God—you would know as much as he does and be as powerful as he is. That's not the kind of God I want. I want a God that is obviously bigger, more powerful and perfect than I am; otherwise, I'm in trouble and you are in trouble. I know some of my own weaknesses and imperfections as I'm sure you know yours. I believe you would agree that a God only equal to me or you would be inadequate."

He nodded his assent while saying, "I never thought of it that way before."

"Secondly," I continued, "on a more positive approach, consider this. As an engineer, think of the finest, best functioning thing you know that is made by human hands. As for me, I know of nothing that can be counted on to last for more than a few years at most. Yet, both of us have observed and know the exact time the sun will rise not only tomorrow morning but also one year and ten years ahead and on into the future, because of the perfectness of the universe that the Bible says God created. This perfectness is used by the scientist. Without the knowledge and use of it no astronaut would dare sit atop a rocket and be blasted off to the moon.

"Consider the reproductive power in seeds and plants on which you and I depend for food, clothing, and shelter. A God of creation had to provide us with these as a starter before our creative talents could be put to use. Consider yourself as a person and the functioning of your entire being. With all our skills we have not created anything so complex, nor have we created life. So when I observe these and many other things about me, I know there has to be an omnipotent God of creation.

"A few say it all resulted from some cosmic accident. Common sense tells me this is impossible because there is no evidence of any perfection resulting from an accident. Some continue to cling to the evolutionary theory—but tell me, even if it were true, who stopped the process where we are, or controlled its rate so that fragile humans could survive? There would still have to be someone, a God, in charge."

Again, Eric nodded his agreement.

"Thirdly," I said, "my own experience of putting my faith and trust in Jesus Christ and what it has done in my life assures me that he is the God of creation, as the Bible also says in the first chapter of John. This is something you, too, can experience by acting as I did." Turning to his daughter, I asked, "If you stood Dianne on the mantel and asked her to jump into your nearby arms, would she do it?"

His response was, "Certainly she would."

I asked, "Why?"

"Because she knows that I'm her father, and from experience and instinct she knows that I will take care of her and not ask her to do something that will hurt her," he said.

And I asked, "On occasions does she do something on her own and get hurt?"

"Oh, yes," Eric responded.

"And as a loving father, you help her to recover from that experience, don't you?" I added. "Don't you see, Eric, that that is a picture of the relationship that God the Father and Creator wants with you and me; and I know that I have with him? He gave us freedom of choice so that we can choose to do wrong and get hurt; but he is always ready to forgive and receive us into his loving care when we turn to him. Actually, life would be meaningless without faith and assurance of something better to look forward to in the future."

Eric thought for a moment and then said, "I'm not sure that I understand everything you have said, but you are making more sense than anyone else has. Enough so that I'll tell you that we will start coming to Bible study and church and give it a try."

As we got up to leave, I reminded Eric that he had made a wise decision and that he, his family, and undoubtedly many others would benefit from it.

Walking to the door, Eric continued, "I should tell you that I don't know why I invited you in when you folks came to the door tonight, but I'm glad I did. Normally I don't let people from the church in."

I said, "The Bible says God works in many and mysterious ways. Let's just say this was one of them."

As we said good-night, Eric asked, "Would you come back sometime when my wife is home? I'd like you to go over with her the same thing you did with me."

"We would be delighted to do it again," was our response.

Eric and his family did come to Bible study and worship as promised, started to grow, became Christians, and joined the church. They participated and continued to grow and serve and had a happier life, as you would expect. Much more could be said about Eric and his family's Christian experiences, but let's stop here and look at it from a different perspective. What does this experience say about Christian discipleship, the role of the church, and the goal of a Christian?

The goal should be to become Christlike, to discover what it means to be in the image of God. The role of the church should be to reach out to people so that they may be reconciled to God and brought into the fellowship of believers and then to nurture and to develop discipleship. Discipleship, then, is to reach out to win and also in love to serve the needs of humanity.

Christ said, "Go." Someone called on Eric. Bible study, worship, fellowship, and service followed to develop in him discipleship and a sensitivity to God. Giving is part of the growth process. The Bible says giving starts after the tithe and involves material possessions and oneself in service.

In summary, the call on Eric is *a demonstration of how to start changing the world!* We must be open to God working through us to change the lives of individual people.

Change the World?

CHAPTER 2

Change the world? Who? Me? Yes, starting with you and me right in our own hometowns.

Mark Twain once said, "To be good is noble; to tell someone else to be good is a lot nobler and a heck of a lot less trouble." My purpose here is not just to tell you how noble you should be, but to help us all to discover who we are and *why* we are here on this earth.

It just may be that the most important thing we will discover is that we don't understand the role we are supposed to play—individually and collectively. This can be illustrated by the story of a sick wife.

This particular wife had been going to the family doctor regularly for some time when the doctor talked privately with the husband to tell him that he could find nothing organically wrong with her. The doctor suggested that the problem was mental and that the husband should take her to a psychiatrist. Being a "good" husband, he made an appointment to take his wife to a psychiatrist. After a few visits the psychiatrist was sure he knew the problem but was having trouble getting the message through to the couple. He developed a strategy to overcome the problem. It involved scheduling their next appointment the next day the first thing in the morning with the doctor in the reception room to greet them as they arrived. As the husband opened the door for his wife to enter, the doctor rushed over to throw his arms around the wife to hug and kiss her. Then stepping back and pointing to the husband, he said, "There, my good man, that is what your wife needs every morning."

"But, doc," the husband protested, "I don't have time to bring her in every morning!"

Obviously the husband did not recognize his proper role in the situation, just as most of us may not recognize that we have a role in changing the world.

All right, what is our role? Who are we? What are we here for? Can we change the world even if we want to? That is a big order—it will take a lot of people who truly understand their role and potential to do good.

Let us start at the beginning by turning to God's word in the first chapter of the first book of the Bible:

> Then God said, "Let us make a man—someone like ourselves, to be the master of all life upon the earth and in the skies and in the seas."
> So God made man like his Maker.
> Like God did God make man;
> Man and maid did he make them.
> And God blessed them and told them, "Multiply and fill the earth and subdue it; you are masters of the fish and birds and all the animals" (Genesis 1:26-28, *The Living Bible*).

Note two tremendous thoughts. First, we are created in God's likeness. This means that each of us has the potential to be like God, and he wants us to be. A fuller meaning of this likeness to God will be discussed in the next chapter.

Second, note that God put us in charge of the rest of his creation. What a responsibility! He expects great things of us. But to develop in his image and have his power available to us, we must exercise our faith as pointed out in 2 Peter 1:5.

The fact that God expects great things of us is also confirmed by the Great Commission, Matthew 28:18-20, where Jesus charged us to go into all the world to make disciples. However, God left us free to choose to be obedient or rebellious to his command. In John 8:32 we are told that we are truly disciples only if we live as he wants us to live. In doing that, we learn God's truth, and the truth sets us free.

Throughout history and continuing today a major concern of people has been freedom. Because of an inadequate relationship to God, people inevitably enslave themselves, a neighbor, or a neighboring society. More on this later.

"But," someone may say, "I want to do what God wants me to—and will—just as soon as *he* shows me what it is." Then a person adds, "My problem is that I just don't know what God wants of me. *He* hasn't spoken to me in a recognizable way yet." Unfortunately, something like Paul's Damascus road experience seems to be what most people expect when God speaks.

I suspect that that is not our *real problem*. I suspect our problem is really one of two things.

First—we have not developed a sensitivity to God that permits us to recognize *him* when *he* speaks in other ways, such as through a pastor, Bible teacher, in a dream, through nature, or otherwise (discussed further in a later chapter). In *The Living Bible* paraphrase of John 7:17 we read, "If any of you really determines to do God's will, then you will certainly know whether my teaching is from God or is merely my own."

Second—we have not established proper priorities for our lives and are holding onto something we should not. To illustrate: A four-year-old lad dropped a penny in a vase while playing in his home. He reached into the vase to get the penny, but then he could not get his hand out. As he walked into the next room where his mother was working, she almost fainted when she saw the lad swinging his arm with the vase stuck on it. The vase was an heirloom that had been handed down through several generations of the family and was considered the mother's most valuable possession. The mother grabbed the four-year-old and tried frantically to remove the vase, but she couldn't. She called her husband home from the office. He could not remove the vase from the arm either. They called the family doctor, because by now the child's wrist was becoming irritated from the effort. The doctor quickly concluded that further effort could possibly damage the lad's wrist permanently and called for a hammer to break the valuable vase. This action caused near hysteria in the parents, whereupon the lad looked up at the doctor and asked, "Would it help any if I let go of the penny?"

You see, his empty hand had entered the vase easily, but when the hand was clenched around the penny, it was too big to pass through the opening. His holding onto the penny almost caused the loss of the valuable vase. And so it often is in our own lives: we hold onto some of our own personal desires instead of reordering our priorities to do God's will.

All of us have priorities, whether stated or not; they are established by the order in which we do things. Jesus clearly had priorities. They fall basically into four categories although many of his words and/or actions can be classified in more than one category.

1. *Proclaim the gospel*

We are told in the Gospels of Matthew, Mark, and Luke that Jesus went about all of Galilee preaching the gospel of the kingdom. The most famous sermon ever delivered was the Sermon on the Mount, which Jesus delivered during his Galilean ministry and which is recorded in both Matthew and Luke.

2. *Choose disciples—persuade others to follow*

Jesus' calling of a tax collector and fishermen as followers and the way he changed their lives are best known. The first twelve disciples are mentioned in Matthew 10 along with his instructions to them. In Luke 10 we are told of an additional seventy. Because of his impending death, it would be through these and future disciples that the gospel would be carried to all parts of the world.

3. *Teach*

There are repeated references to Jesus' extensive teaching ministry. We are told that he taught daily in the temple and on many special occasions, such as the Feast of Tabernacles and the Feast of Dedication. He regularly was teaching the disciples in the ministry. He taught them how to pray, and we have the example known as the Lord's Prayer. We are also told of his teaching the multitudes. One of his favorite methods was the use of parables.

4. *Heal*

Jesus' healing ministry was extensive and included overcoming death, disease, physical defects, and mental and spiritual problems. He healed lepers, the blind, the crippled, the demoniac, and many more. He overcame death himself as well as restoring life to Lazarus, the daughter of Jairus, and the son of the widow of Nain. Importantly, he empowered his disciples to do likewise.

We would do well to consider these priorities ourselves, because if the world is to be changed, it must start by changing individuals; and we don't have to quit our jobs and go to the seminary to do it. Nor do we have to be offensive and pious. We've just got to show by our lives, wherever we are, that the things of God and the church are important—*High Priority.*

James 2:20 tells us that faith without works is dead—no faith at all. And Romans 8:28 tells us that all things are possible if we are working within God's plans.

So you see, the real question is not the one posed earlier: "Can we change the world even if we want to?" The real question is: *"Do we want to?"*

As for me, I am not ready to give up on the church as an instrument to change the world. The church has, perhaps, the greatest opportunity in its history if we as its members are creative and faithful in our work. To illustrate how to be creative, I like the story of the local community grocer.

The grocer, located in the middle of the block, saw buildings torn down on one side of his store and a new supermarket go up, after which he lost much of his business. Then the same thing started on the other side of his store. The local grocer was better prepared for the opening of the second supermarket. He had prepared and installed a large sign over the entrance to his store. It said simply *MAIN ENTRANCE.*

My challenge to every reader is that you personally will commit yourself to the work of Christ's church so faithfully that you will help revitalize your own church and point the way for many to the main entrance into the changed world of a happy life through faith in Jesus Christ, as well as membership, study, service, and fellowship in and through the local church.

In God's Image

CHAPTER 3

We Christians generally do not understand our potential for doing good—serving God. As mentioned briefly in the preceding chapter, perhaps it is because we do not truly understand who we really are and why we are here and therefore do not claim the wisdom and power that is available to us. This lack of understanding has not been helped by the thoughts of many noted mathematicians, scientists, or even theologians. Bertrand Russell claimed that the whole universe was simply the result of an accident, and "only on the firm foundation of unyielding despair can the soul's habitation be safely built."[1] The astronomer Sir Fred Hoyle expressed the view that there is "scarcely a clue [that] our existence has any real significance."[2] And Kierkegaard, a noted religious thinker, asked: "Where am I? Who am I? How came I here? What is this thing called the world? And if I am compelled to take part in it, where is the director?"[3]

This suggests insufficient Christian education or Bible

[1] E. F. Schumacher, *Small Is Beautiful* (New York: Harper Torchbooks, imprint of Harper & Row, Publishers, 1973), p. 78.
[2] *Ibid.*
[3] *Ibid.*

study since the message is spread throughout the Bible—from Genesis to Revelation. I like E. F. Schumacher's definition of education—"the transmission of ideas which enable [people] to choose between one thing and another, or, to quote Ortega . . ., 'to live a life which is something above meaningless tragedy or inward disgrace.'"[4]

Let's do some Bible study then to shed further light on the question of who we are and why we are here. It starts with Genesis 1:26-29.

> And God said, Let us make man in our image, after our likeness: and let them have dominion over the fish of the sea, and over the fowl of the air, and over the cattle, and over all the earth, and over every creeping thing that creepeth upon the earth. So God created man in his own image, in the image of God created he him; male and female created he them.

I particularly like *The Living Bible* paraphrase which says: "Let us make a man—someone like ourselves. . . ." Perhaps we can start comprehending the greatness of this thought if we completely put out of our minds any thought of physical image or likeness and concentrate on the characteristics of God as we find them in the Bible. Here are only some of them. God is creative—compassionate—faithful—powerful—good—glorious—fatherly—holy—impartial—infinite— knowledgeable—long-suffering—merciful—righteous—unchangeable—perfect—true—sovereign—and God is love.

We'll look at a few of the references that tell us this, but first, think about it: God wants us to be like him and created us so that we can be if we use the freedom of choice he gave us to choose, with his help, to grow toward the perfection which is in him.

Looking at Genesis 1:28, we can see the wisdom of God in making this possible. He put man and woman, his greatest creations, in charge of all else he created. What a responsibility!

[4] *Ibid.*, p. 79.

26

In addition to the verses quoted previously, the entire first chapter of Genesis deals with the creative acts of God. In John 1:1-3 (TLB) the Christ is also related to God and creation: "Before anything else existed, there was Christ, with God. He has always been alive and is himself God. He created everything there is—nothing exists that he didn't make." Consider Psalm 8:3-6: "When I consider thy heavens, the work of thy fingers, the moon and the stars, which thou hast ordained; what is man, that thou art mindful of him? And the son of man, that thou visitest him? For thou has made him a little lower than the angels, and hast crowned him with glory and honour. Thou madest him to have dominion over the works of thy hands; thou hast put all things under his feet." Note Proverbs 22:2 (RSV): "The rich and poor meet together; the Lord is the maker of them all" and Malachi 2:10a: "Have we not all one father? hath not one God created us?"

Surely God wants us to make creative discoveries while *wisely* using and having dominion over the creations God gave us from his initial works. It should come as no surprise that creative developments in the world continue at an unprecedented rate. We are supposed to develop our creative characteristics. Neither should it come as a surprise that all developments are not always used for the good of society, because of inadequate development of the wisdom needed for proper use of these creative acts. To do so, we must develop and claim the other characteristics of God that are potentially ours by being made in *his image.*

There is great debate in society about the "right" of people to utilize the resources of God's creation. There is too little discussion in the church designed to help us to function in the image of God—a little lower than the angels. If there were more discussion, there would be less doubt about proper utilization of the rest of God's creation for the good of God's greatest creation—man and woman. Guidance is possible if we recognize the great resource available to us: "The Lord is nigh unto all them that call upon him, to all that call upon him in truth" (Psalm 145:18). "Let us therefore come boldly unto the throne of grace, that we may obtain mercy, and find grace to help in time of need" (Hebrews 4:16). "But without faith it is impossible to please him: for he that cometh to God must believe that he is, and that he is a rewarder of them that diligently seek him" (Hebrews 11:6).

Persons who have developed creatively, whether as scientists, engineers, or artists, have great confidence in their ability to achieve their purpose. The same persons do not always include as part of their purpose the pleasing of God. Certainly we have a time of need now and must learn to come boldly to God for the answer to our need.

If we were faithful in diligently seeking God's help, we would develop another characteristic of God—*faithfulness.* "Ye know in all your hearts and all your souls, that not one thing hath failed of all the good things which the Lord your God spake concerning you; all are come to pass unto you, and not one thing hath failed thereof" (Joshua 23:14). "God is faithful, who will not suffer you to be tempted above that ye are able" (1 Corinthians 10:13). "If we confess our sins, he is faithful and just to forgive us our sins, and to cleanse us from all unrighteousness" (1 John 1:9). "For thou, Lord, art good, and ready to forgive; and plenteous in mercy unto all them that call upon thee" (Psalm 86:5). "The Lord is good, a strong hold in the day of trouble" (Nahum 1:7). "Every good gift and every perfect gift is from above, and cometh down from the Father of lights" (James 1:17).

Most people recognize that the world has a whole variety of troubles, but apparently too few recognize the truth from Nahum that the Lord is a stronghold in the day of trouble. How unlikely it is that society will recognize this truth as long as the great religions, including Christianity, set the examples they now do! Christians and Moslems slaughter one another in Lebanon, as do Catholics and Protestants in Ireland. Jews and Moslems kill each other in the Mideast and at airports and Olympic games elsewhere in the world. Hardly any group can truly say, "Follow our example—confess your sins to God, wipe the slate clean, and claim the good and perfect gift from above that is so desperately needed." So from the Scripture references given and hundreds of other passages we find that God is a good and gracious giver of gifts.

There is something else that we should aspire to be. God is also a holy God. See Leviticus 19:2, "Ye shall be holy: for I the Lord your God am holy"; Isaiah 6:3, "Holy, holy, holy, is the Lord of hosts: the whole earth is full of his glory"; and 1 Peter 1:15-16, "But as he which hath called you is holy, so be ye holy in all manner of conversation; because it is written, Be ye holy; for I am holy."

Even among Christian church members there is a great tendency to apologize for any symptom of holiness. You probably have heard, as I have, someone say something to the effect of "I don't want to seem pious or appear holier than thou." If we are to develop in God's image and give leadership to others, then our lives must show some holy qualities. These should be shown by our actions, *not* by our proclamations.

God is also knowledgeable, long-suffering, merciful, and loving. "The Lord is a God of knowledge, and by him actions are weighed" (1 Samuel 2:3). "But I know thy abode, and thy going out, and thy coming in, and thy rage against me" (Isaiah 37:28). "The Lord is not slack concerning his promise, as some men count slackness; but is longsuffering to us-ward, not willing that any should perish, but that all should come to repentance" (2 Peter 3:9). "God loveth a cheerful giver" (2 Corinthians 9:7).

It is evident that a segment of Christianity and some other religions believe that intellectual accomplishments and special abilities are incompatible with being merciful and long-suffering. Sackcloth and ashes too often come from an unwillingness to develop and use the talents God gave us rather than *willingly give our all.* Albert Schweitzer, one who *did* willingly give his all, is a prominent example of many who could be named from many walks of life over a long period of time. He developed the talents God gave him and then in the name of Christ gave them all to the less fortunate.

Perhaps the best-known verse in the Bible that says it all about God's love and giving is "God so loved the world, that he gave his only begotten Son, that whosoever believeth in him should not perish, but have everlasting life" (John 3:16). See also Numbers 14:18, "The Lord is longsuffering, and of great mercy, forgiving iniquity and transgression"; Psalm 111:4, "The Lord is gracious and full of compassion"; Matthew 6:14, "If ye forgive men their trespasses, your heavenly Father will also forgive you"; and Luke 6:36, "Be ye therefore merciful, as your Father also is merciful."

But we are likely to say to ourselves, "If that is what being in the image of God means, I may as well forget it—there is no way." Certainly we can agree that we will not be perfect as he is perfect, but we can try, and we can want to be like him—and we can be a lot better and more effective than we are if we remember that God is powerful and the source of our salvation. "He hath shewed his people the power of his works" (Psalm 111:6). "With God all things are possible" (Matthew 19:26). "Unto him that is able to do exceeding abundantly above all that we ask or think, according to the power that worketh in us, unto him be glory in the church by Christ Jesus throughout all ages, world without end" (Ephesians 3:20-21). "Thou shalt know no god but me: for there is no saviour beside me" (Hosea 13:4). "I am not ashamed of the gospel of Christ: for it is the power of God unto salvation to every one that believeth . . ." (Romans 1:16).

So if you want to be happy and able to deal with the problems of life, then remember who you are (a creation of God in his image) and why you are here (to do God's will), and claim the promises of God that have been proven true. To do so, you must recognize God when he speaks to you, and one sure way to start is by speaking to God.

We must also recognize the need for continued spiritual growth. The whole process is outlined in Second Peter, chapter 1, verses 1 through 8 and is discussed in chapter 5 of this book.

Some of the Ways God Speaks to Us

CHAPTER 4

The following poem first appeared in the *Becker County Record,* Detroit Lakes, Minnesota. It was picked up by the U.S. Press Association and passed along to its subscribers. The poem was found on the body of a nineteen-year-old soldier in Vietnam.

Look, God: I have never spoken to you, but now—
I want to say: "How do you do?"
You see, God, they told me you didn't exist
And like a fool—I believed all of this.
Last night from a shell-hole I saw your sky—
Figured right then they had told me a lie.
Had I taken the time to see the things you made,
I'd know they weren't calling a spade a spade.
I wonder, God, if you'd shake my hand.
Somehow—I feel you will understand.
Funny, I had to come to this hellish place
Before I had time to see your face.
Well, I guess there isn't much more to say.
But I'm sure glad, God, I met you today.

I guess the zero-hour will soon be here.
But I'm not afraid since I know you are here.
The signal—well, God—I'll have to go,
I like you lots—this I want you to know.
Looks like this will be a horrible fight.
Who knows—I may come to your house tonight.
Though I wasn't friendly with you before,
I wonder, God—if you'd wait at your door.
Look—I'm crying, me shedding tears,
I wish I'd known you these many years.
Well, I'll have to go now, God—good-bye.
Strange—since I met you—
I'm not afraid to die.

The Bible teaches that God is ever-present, trying to speak to and lead us in the way that is best. This young soldier learned this just as Jacob did centuries earlier as revealed in Genesis 28:16 (RSV), "Then Jacob awoke from his sleep and said: 'Surely the Lord is in this place; and I did not know it.'"

34

Surely one of our major objectives as Christians should be to develop our own—and help others to develop—awareness of the omnipresence of God and the various ways he may use to speak to us.

These ways generally may be classified under four headings:

(1) God speaks directly to people: for example, as Jesus Christ did in his first-century ministry or through the Holy Spirit subsequently and now.
(2) God speaks through the written Word, the Bible.
(3) God speaks through his creation that is all around us.
(4) God speaks through people—through the pastor of a church, a Bible teacher, or ordinary people and events in history.

We can gain valuable insights and evidence on each of

these ways that God speaks by selecting only a few of the many references on each found in the Bible.

Throughout the Old Testament and into the New we have examples of God speaking in a variety of ways directly to people. The following passages confirm this. Many individuals can confirm that God continues to do the same today.

> In many and various ways God spoke of old to our fathers by the prophets; but in these last days he has spoken to us by a Son, whom he appointed the heir of all things, through whom also he created the world (Hebrews 1:1-2, RSV).

Moses, Noah, Daniel, Jacob, Samuel, and many others of the Old Testament experienced God speaking directly with them. Thousands experienced the very personalized ministry of God through Jesus Christ; and the Holy Spirit speaks today, just as Paul and Peter experienced it.

In the process of making over five thousand calls in homes on behalf of the church and the cause of Christ, I've encountered numerous situations that required answers for which I was not prepared but which were furnished by the Holy Spirit when I was receptive. The first chapter of this book is a specific illustration.

God's Spirit has also led me in business decisions on many occasions when, though sufficient information was not available, there was a need for and a desire to make the right decision. This has been particularly evident in giving help and leadership to associates and perhaps accounts for many seeking me out to discuss personal matters—matters which require talking to someone they can trust.

> So we must listen very carefully to the truths we have heard, or we may drift away from them. For since the messages from angels have always proved true and people have always been punished for disobeying them, what makes us think that we can escape if we are indifferent to this great salvation announced by the Lord Jesus himself, and passed on to us by those who heard him speak? (Hebrews 2:1-3, TLB).

God always has shown us that these messages are true by means of signs and wonders and various miracles and by giving certain *special abilities* from the Holy Spirit to those who believe; yes, God has assigned such gifts to each of us.

It is my belief that all of my abilities are a gift from God; but he has given me a special ability to help young people in business to see that, by discovering who they really are and developing their latent talents, they are capable of becoming more than they think they can. All of us have observed others that seemed to "excel" in a particular thing or two—they have special talents.

What a tragedy that so many go through life and never discover their own "gifts" because they never become sensitive to God's speaking and leading! What a tragedy also that when special gifts are mentioned, so many Christians seem to think of things like speaking in tongues instead of things more useful. Paul cautioned against this type of thinking and, to emphasize it, listed speaking in tongues last when talking about special gifts. Paul, in writing to the early churches, said that his own experiences confirmed what the Scriptures teach about God speaking to us.

> But, as it is written,
> "What no eye has seen, nor ear heard,
> nor the heart of man conceived,
> what God has prepared for those who love him,"
> God has revealed to us through the Spirit. For the Spirit searches everything, even the depths of God (1 Corinthians 2:9-10, RSV).

> Dear friends, I solemnly swear that the way to heaven which I preach is not based on some mere human whim or dream. For my message comes from no less a person than Jesus Christ himself, who told me what to say. No one else has taught me (Galatians 1:11-12, TLB).

John says that God's message of love isn't just something he's read about but something he's seen and heard personally (1

John 1:1). On two separate occasions, when one of our children had polio as a baby and another had a brain tumor at age twenty-nine, both my wife and I experienced a comforting peace of mind after the initial shock of the doctor's diagnoses. We can say with Paul and John that God's love is something we know personally and of which we have proof.

> And Christ became a human being and lived here on earth among us and was full of loving forgiveness and truth. And some of us have seen his glory—the glory of the only Son of the heavenly Father! (John 1:14, TLB).

And Peter says it wasn't just an illusion—we believers have proof.

> So we have seen and proved that what the prophets said came true. You will do well to pay close attention to everything they have written, for, like lights shining into dark corners, their words help us to understand many things that otherwise would be dark and difficult. But when you consider the wonderful truth of the prophets' words, then the light will dawn in your souls and Christ the Morning Star will shine in your hearts. For no prophecy recorded in Scripture was ever thought up by the prophet himself. It was the Holy Spirit within these godly men who gave them true messages from God (2 Peter 1:19-21, TLB).

In the story of Lazarus and the rich man, found in the sixteenth chapter of Luke, God says if we won't accept proof given by others (Moses or the prophets), then we wouldn't accept it in any way, even if someone rose from the dead to tell us. Solely on the basis of someone else's understanding, we so readily accept and use scientific truths that we don't understand. It is sad that the greater spiritual truths are not equally accepted.

> "But always, first of all, I warn you through my prophets. This I now have done" (Amos 3:7, TLB).

The Bible as the inspired Word of God is a most important way that God speaks to us—not only in revealing himself but in giving us guidelines for daily living.

In Philippians 2 Paul speaks of Christ's ministry, his own, and that of his associates and urges those of the church at Philippi to be like-minded because "it is God which worketh in you both to will and to do of his good pleasure."

Talented people especially need to hear this message and example of Paul and give credit to God for their talents and accomplishments.

In Ephesians 4, in addition to giving instructions on what to and not to do in living our lives, Paul points out that God calls each Christian but that his or her service may be in different capacities. It is the same and only God working through each for a common purpose: the perfecting of the saints for the work of the ministry and a unity of faith and knowledge of the Son of God. People need to feel "called" to be businessmen, government workers, pastors, and all honorable professions. I do feel called, but I believe many people go through life unhappy and frustrated in their work because of a lack of understanding of their call.

In 1 Corinthians 13—known as the great "love" chapter— in verse 12 Paul points out that now we don't always see clearly or wholly understand, but ultimately we will be face to face with God and will understand fully. This again places emphasis on the need for faith. God will never prove everything to our satisfaction. To do so would place us in the role of God, and think what a tragedy that would be!

In Exodus, we see the raising up of a leader (Moses) of a people and the detailed communications of God to these people through Moses, who was chosen because of his sensitivity to God and a willingness to serve God (after a reluctant start). Perhaps what our country needs most are elected leaders who openly develop this kind of relationship with God. I am sure God offers it just as he did with Moses.

There is so much in creation all about us that speaks so completely of an omnipotent God for any who will see—the vastness and precision of the universe; the power of the storm and the tiny seed; the beauty of the flower; the complexities and functioning of all living creation, including human beings.

> But God shows his anger from heaven against all sinful, evil men who push away the truth from them. For the truth about God is known to them instinctively; God has put this knowledge in their hearts. Since earliest times men have seen the earth and sky and all God made, and have known of his existence and great eternal power. So they will have no excuse [when they stand before God at Judgment Day].
> Yes, they knew about him all right, but they wouldn't admit it or worship him or even thank him for all his daily care. And after awhile they began to think up silly ideas of what God was like and what he wanted them to do. The result was that their foolish minds became dark and confused (Romans 1:18–21, TLB).

My experience confirms Paul's statement. It is incomprehensible to me that any intelligent person can observe nature around us and be unaware of the existence of a higher being— God. The following passage from the Psalms confirms that God is speaking to us without using a word or sound. Statements from a number of our astronauts who have been in space also seem to confirm it.

> The heavens are telling the glory of God; they are a marvelous display of his craftsmanship. Day and night they keep on telling about God. Without a sound or word, silent in the skies, their message reaches out to all the world . . . (Psalm 19:1–4, TLB).

It is not sufficient for us just to be aware of God's existence through use of our intelligence in observing his magnificent creation. We must have faith in God. In the following passage from Titus, Paul says he has been trusted to help bring this about. I believe that this probably applies also to all Christians.

> From: Paul, the slave of God and the messenger of Jesus Christ.
> I have been sent to bring faith to those God has chosen and

to teach them to know God's truth—the kind of truth that changes lives—so that they can have eternal life, which God promised them before the world began—and he cannot lie. And now in his own good time he has revealed this Good News and permits me to tell it to everyone. By command of God our Savior I have been trusted to do this work for him (Titus 1:1-3, TLB).

Just in case we are inclined to take this responsibility too lightly, as most of us probably are, the following passage from Hebrews should remind us not only of the gifts God has given us but also of the hazard of not listening to God's leading that we may fully develop these gifts through service.

So we must listen very carefully to the truths we have heard, or we may drift away from them. For since the messages from angels have always proved true and people have always been punished for disobeying them, what makes us think that we can escape if we are indifferent to this great salvation announced by the Lord Jesus himself, and passed on to us by those who heard him speak?

God always has shown us that these messages are true by signs and wonders and various miracles and by giving certain special abilities from the Holy Spirit to those who believe; yes, God has assigned such gifts to each of us (Hebrews 2:1-4, TLB).

Could there be a better case made for the need for our diligence in continuing to learn and grow as Christians? Without this growth our perspective and understanding of events and how to deal with them can be totally wrong. A good illustration is the life of Joseph and the relationship with his brothers, as found in the Old Testament. In Pharaoh's court the brothers recalled their horrible deed.

Speaking among themselves, they said, "This has all happened because of what we did to Joseph long ago. We saw his terror and anguish and heard his pleadings, but we wouldn't listen" (Genesis 42:21, TLB).

But the view of Joseph, God's servant, in the reunion with his brothers, as found in Genesis 45:1-13, was that God uses many and varied situations to accomplish his purpose, as stated in verse 8: "So now it was not you that sent me hither, but God. . . ."

People seriously trying to serve God are able, with his leading, to make the most of a situation. Too often, we tend to complain and criticize.

Even when our choices are wrong, as were Joseph's brothers, God can and will use the event for good—provided there is a willing servant, as was Joseph. One of the great principles of Dale Carnegie's success was to turn a liability into an asset by thinking positively about a situation. Thinking positively is not "operation shoestring" but utilizing for good all the talent with which God endowed us and turning to God as our guide for decision making.

In Deuteronomy 11 we learn of the good that happens when we listen to and heed God's commandments when he speaks to us and that woe which we bring upon ourselves when we fail to heed God's leading. Obviously we will never be perfect in heeding God's will, but fortunately a way has been provided to clear the deck and start anew when we recognize our failure.

But now God has shown us a different way to heaven—not by "being good enough" and trying to keep his laws, but by a new way (though not new, really, for the Scriptures told about it long ago). Now God says he will accept and acquit us—declare us "not guilty"—if we trust Jesus Christ to take away our sins. And we all can be saved in this same way, by coming to Christ, no matter who we are or what we have been like. Yes, all have sinned; all fall short of God's glorious ideal; yet now God declares us "not guilty" of offending him if we trust in Jesus Christ, who in his kindness freely takes away our sins.

For God sent Christ Jesus to take the punishment for our sins and to end all God's anger against us. He used Christ's blood and our faith as the means of saving us from his wrath. In this way he was being entirely fair, even though he did not punish those who sinned in former times. For he was looking forward to the time when Christ would come and take away those sins (Romans 3:21-25, TLB).

But continue thou in the things which thou hast learned and hast been assured of, knowing of whom thou hast learned them; and that from a child thou hast known the holy scriptures, which are able to make thee wise unto salvation through faith which is in Christ Jesus. All scripture is given by inspiration of God, and is profitable for doctrine, for reproof, for correction, for instruction in righteousness: that the man of God may be perfect, throughly furnished unto all good works (2 Timothy 3:14-17).

Paul is calling young Timothy's attention to two ways that the knowledge of God is transmitted to people in order that people may grow toward perfection, that is, being in God's image. Knowledge of God is transmitted both from one life to another, as from teacher to pupil, and through the Holy Scriptures into which God has breathed his Spirit.

Churches that do not maintain an effective Bible study program through a church school are missing this point. The church school has meant so much in the stability of my own life, and its influence has also been strongly evident in our children's lives on more than one occasion. My wife and I went to church school for Bible study each Sunday with our children from the time they were babies until they were old enough to leave home. Each of our four children has now had enough experience in life as an adult to confirm that this practice was best for all of us.

The book of Isaiah the prophet was handed to him, and he opened it to the place where it says:
"The Spirit of the Lord is upon me; he has appointed me to preach Good News to the poor; he has sent me . . . to announce that captives shall be released and the blind shall see, that the downtrodden shall be freed from their oppressors, and that God is ready to give blessings to all who come to him" (Luke 4:17-19, TLB).

Jesus set the pattern and established the importance of Bible study. I have never heard an effective argument against it, except the problem of poorly prepared teachers. This problem could be resolved if those who enlist teachers properly communicated the great importance of the job and some of the principles being discussed here.

> And another time when he appeared to them, they asked him, "Lord, are you going to free Israel [from Rome] now and restore us as an independent nation?"
> "The Father sets those dates," he replied, "and they are not for you to know. But when the Holy Spirit has come upon you, you will receive power to testify about me with great effect, to the people in Jerusalem, throughout Judea, in Samaria, and to the ends of the earth, about my death and resurrection" (Acts 1:6-8, TLB).

Almost every year, somewhere in the United States or the world, one or more groups of people establish a date and isolate themselves to await Christ's return. How contradictory to the Scriptures and what a waste of time that could otherwise be used in a ministry to someone! To me this effort points up something very important if we are to be open and receptive to God's speaking to us through the Bible. It is important not to predetermine what we are looking for and want to find, because it seems to me that such an approach is trying to use God instead of letting him use us.

From this study of the Bible we see that God has given us many illustrations of how he speaks to us. We should then be wise enough to understand the need for us to grow and develop a sensitivity to God that will permit us to recognize him when he speaks. This comes from Bible study, prayer, worship, and service. It may be illustrated in the following manner. Take your right forefinger nail and gently scratch the back of your left hand. Note the momentary discoloration as you scratch, which immediately disappears when the scratching stops. Now visualize what would happen if you continued the process for one or two hours. Undoubtedly, the skin would break, and because bacteria probably are under your nail, within twenty-four hours your hand would be inflamed, red, and sore—highly sensitive to touch.

This process illustrates what continuous and regular Bible study, prayer, worship, and service do to the mind and soul of a man or woman. They develop a sensitivity to God's presence. The occasional action, such as church attendance at Easter, represents the first picture. It is obvious that something has occurred, but there is likely to be no lasting effect.

Let's face it—God rarely uses a dramatic way to gain our attention, such as Paul's Damascus road experience; so why not use the intelligence he gave us to prepare for whatever approach he may use? There are many examples in the Bible that serve as insights to guide us—Moses, Noah, Joseph, John, and more. As in any endeavor, preparation is the wisest approach.

How Can One Be Sure It Is God Speaking?

CHAPTER 5

Having developed an awareness and having gained an understanding of the way God speaks to us as discussed in chapter 4 is not enough to develop good communication with God anymore than reading a book on how to play baseball will get anyone to the major leagues.

Reading the book to gain a mental understanding may be a good start, but much more is needed. Motivation is needed— a real desire to want to know and do God's will. Discipline is also needed—the discipline to exercise our faith and talents that we may grow spiritually. The ballplayer or musician not only must want to be good but also must practice to become good. Likewise, we Christians must develop a sensitivity to God so that when he speaks, we will know it is God and will listen and follow.

Jesus, in responding to a criticism, said in John 7:17 (*The Amplified Bible*), "If any man desires to do His will (God's pleasure), he will know—have the needed illumination to recognize, can tell for himself—whether the teaching is from God, or whether I am speaking from Myself and of My own accord and on My own authority." So the first and essential step is really to want to know and do God's will for our lives.

How do we develop this sensitivity to God that will help us to recognize him and understand when he speaks? Bible study, worship, fellowship, prayer, and service are some of the ways. In 2 Peter 1:3-8 we find a beautiful picture of what we need to do to grow spiritually. Note verses 3 and 4 as they appear in *The Amplified Bible:*

> For His divine power has bestowed upon us all things that [are requisite and suited] to life and godliness, through the (full, personal) knowledge of Him Who called us by and to His own glory and excellence (virtue). By means of these He has bestowed on us His precious and exceedingly great promises, so that through them you may escape (by flight) from the moral decay (rottenness and corruption) that is in the world because of covetousness (lust and greed), and become sharers (partakers) of the divine nature.

Note especially that our cup of life must be emptied of the bad things of life before we can grow and have our cup filled with the good things God promises to share. Often we are unwilling to give up pleasures that we do not recognize as being temporary.

> For this very reason, adding your diligence [to the divine promises], employ every effort in exercising your faith to develop virtue (excellence, resolution, Christian energy); and in [exercising] virtue [develop] knowledge (intelligence) (2 Peter 1:5, *The Amplified Bible).*

God does not impose spiritual growth on us. He makes it available but requires us to be dedicated to growth and continually striving to attain it. Great evangelists like Billy Graham, pastors and teachers like John A. Lavender, and governmental leaders like Abraham Lincoln all stated publicly the difficulties they had to overcome to succeed in their calling. The effort and diligence each employed are well documented as is the excellence and knowledge each attained.

Developing knowledge is a continuous and lifetime

assignment; yet our society seemingly has assigned a period of life known as the "school years" and locations known as "institutions of learning" as the time and places to gain knowledge. When we limit the process to this framework, God's promises cannot be delivered in full. Someone has said that a little knowledge is a dangerous thing; perhaps it is dangerous because it may bring conceit. The late President Harry S. Truman said, "Conceit is God's gift to little men."

In the company for which I work we have a continuing education program for our people. Its primary objective *is not* management methods, techniques, or data. Its purpose is to develop a continuing desire to read and study so that there may be a continuing awareness of the environment of the world in which decisions must be made.

> And in [exercising] knowledge [develop] self-control; and in [exercising] self-control [develop] steadfastness (patience, endurance), and in [exercising] steadfastness [develop] godliness (piety), and in [exercising] godliness [develop] brotherly affection, and in [exercising] brotherly affection [develop] Christian love. For as these qualities are yours and increasingly abound in you, they will keep [you] from being idle or unfruitful unto the (full personal) knowledge of our Lord Jesus Christ, the Messiah, the Anointed One (2 Peter 1:6-8, *The Amplified Bible*).

47

Notice that it is necessary for us to add our own diligence to the things with which God has already provided us. Then, just as a baseball player must exercise the physical and mental tools that God has provided to become a good fielder, runner, batter, etc.; so must we exercise our faith to develop virtue which, in turn, we must use to succeed in developing other Christian characteristics necessary to grow in the likeness of God.

Have you ever noticed in a debate that it is the less knowledgeable person who is likely to lose self-control, which then brings more heat than light to a subject? The knowledgeable person, who has self-control, is likely to have the patience to see something successfully through. The most effective businessman I have ever been associated with exemplifies these characteristics.

Now throw in some piety (I don't know why this seems to be avoided so much) and brotherly love, and great progress has been made in developing in the image of God. People with these characteristics are going to be productively busy people—not idle. Look around you—they are easily identified.

When we strive to grow in this way, there is likely to be little doubt in our minds about God speaking to us or what he is saying. We are also likely to become people about whom it is said, "I don't see how they get so much done." The unseen helper and guiding wisdom is likely to be the God of great promises.

The story of the Pittron Company of Glassport, Pennsylvania, is a great illustration of the message of this chapter, as well as other points of this book.

A foundry operation that had been best known for labor strife and unprofitability for most of its history turned around on both counts during the early 1970s. This happened because the general manager of operations, Wayne Alderson, felt led of God to start a Bible study at the plant during the lunch hour. He also had a deep interest and concern for his fellow workers. While the plan was met with skepticism by workers and other management at first, it succeeded, and dramatically so, as the Bible study and fellowship led to growth and understanding on the part of all.

A television documentary of the Pittron story has just been completed. It confirms the growth philosophy outlined in this chapter and also that, indeed, *one person does make a difference* for good when he or she is sensitive to God's leading.

The Church: Leader or Critic?

CHAPTER 6

There is much to suggest that the church has lost its position of leadership in society, a position the church—as individual members and as an institution—has held for centuries. Why? Why, at a time when the need and opportunity for leadership are so great, does the church seem to have assumed the role of chief critic of society? Is this a proper and/or complete role for the church? How does the church differ in its makeup from other institutions of society as an institution made up of individuals? Why can't we as individuals and institutions get together on some common goals? Let's look at some comparisons and possible reasons.

We have become a push-button society. We push a button or flip a switch, and lights come on, motors start, food cooks, and all kinds of things happen—instantly. This has brought comfort and convenience to millions and relieved humankind of much drudgery. Such instant action has made it possible for people to have time for and to make choices about more fulfilling activities. There is also much evidence that it can result in the opposite, if improperly used.

It has also caused something else to happen that is not

adequately recognized. It has led to a "shorthand" type of conversation that starts from insufficient or no facts, is carried out in generalizations, and uses words that have different meanings to different people. We seem to think that thirty minutes of television news is sufficient to inform us of all the world's activities.

We don't take the time to research for fact; we assume that because something has been put in print, or on radio or TV, it is fact. Then we proceed to use labels—Government, Business, Corporations, Unions, the Church, Education, the Home—as umbrella words for large segments of society; and if a few individuals in any segment make unwise choices and do wrong, then all people under that umbrella label are classified the same way.

We in the church, and particularly professional church leadership, rightfully talk a lot about the dignity of persons. At the same time we violate this principle perhaps more than any other group by not looking at, working with, and being forgiving of individuals as we try to change the world.

It is common rhetoric for church and educational leaders to condemn business corporations. Sometimes the acts of individual business leaders are deserving of condemnation. But so is the act of an individual professional church leader who steals another man's wife or sells securities fraudulently to raise funds. The same can be said for a government, education, or union leader who violates a trust. Shifting a responsibility from one institution to another gives no assurance of correcting a problem, unless there is evidence that the people in one institution are more receptive to God's leading than those in another. And the world seems to be saying to the church, "Heal yourself before doctoring me; demonstate your worthiness to lead before asking me to follow."

Perhaps most of us have lost sight of, or have never understood, what true leadership entails. Robert K. Greenleaf in *The Servant as Leader* [1] has captured in words a vision of leadership that is worthy of the thoughtful consideration of all of us.

A fresh critical look is being taken at the issues of power and authority, and people are beginning to learn, however haltingly, to relate to one another in less coercive and more creatively supporting ways. A new moral principle is emerging which holds that the only authority deserving one's allegiance is that which is freely and knowingly granted by the led to the leader in response to, and in proportion to, the clearly evident servant stature of the leader. Those who choose to follow this principle will not casually accept the authority of existing institutions. *Rather, they will freely respond only to individuals who are chosen as leaders because they are proven and trusted as servants.* To the extent that this principle prevails in the future, the only viable institutions will be those that are predominantly servant-led. And with this we hope there will be an openness of style in which leaders will be natural men acting naturally, mortal men subject to error and deserving forgiveness like everybody else.

. . . . Enough trust to hold a society together, so that the impossible can be made possible, will not issue full-blown simply because it is demanded. Those who strongly feel the need must do the hard work, the disciplined serving and leading that are necessary to bring it about. . . . Builders must emerge from among the critics if the present ferment is to produce a better society. . . .

. . . . The servant-leader is not necessarily the most popular among his contemporaries. The "popular" leader type will very likely gravitate to easier alternatives to choose. Among them is the assumption that since the effort to reform existing institutions has not brought perfection, the remedy is to destroy them completely so that fresh, new, perfect ones can grow. Not much thought seems to be given to the problem of where the new seed will come from or who the gardener to tend it will be.

Serving stands in sharp contrast to this kind of thinking. It requires that the concerned individual accept the problems he sees in the world as his own personal task, as a means of achieving his own integrity. He sees the external manifestation of this internal achievement as beginning with caring for individual persons in ways that require dedication and skill and that help them grow and become

51

[1] Taken from Robert K. Greenleaf, *The Servant as Leader* (Cambridge, Mass.: Center for Applied Studies, 1970, 1973). Copyright by Robert K. Greenleaf. Reproduced by permission.

wealthier, stronger, and more autonomous. The servant will move from this to larger spheres of influence, leading and showing the way to larger groups—institutions, perhaps—vast culture-shaping institutions. One consequence of the contemporary revolution, as I see it, is that there will not be enough trust in any other kind of leader to make a viable society possible. . . .

Serving (and leading as so defined) is not popular, because it is exacting and hard to attain. But it is highly rewarding and fulfilling when it is done well. . . . Criticism has its place; but as a total preoccupation it is sterile. In a time of crisis, . . . if too many potential builders are taken in by a complete absorption with dissecting the wrong and by a zeal for instant perfection, then the future of this civilization is dark indeed. The danger, perhaps, is to hear the analyst too much and the artist too little. . . . The healthy society, like the healthy body, is not the one that has taken the most medicine. It is the one in which the internal health building forces are in the best shape.

The real enemy is fuzzy thinking on the part of good, intelligent, vital people, and their failure to lead. . . . Too many settle for being critics and experts. . . . *In short, the enemy is . . . servants who have the potential to lead but do not lead.* . . .

This concept of leadership outlined by Greenleaf has been demonstrated by a number of individuals in a variety of situations. It certainly should not be new to the Christian church. The ministry of Jesus Christ was a demonstration of servanthood; he was a servant-leader.

The following is an example of leadership on the subject of ethics and morality as it pertains to the industrial corporation in the United States today. This letter was sent to all employees by the chairman of the company with which I work.[2]

My associates in management:

The continuing revelations of what is alleged to be improper conduct by employees of private companies and corporations have created an environment of distrust of private enterprise. Allegations have run the gamut from illegal acts such as use of corporate funds for political contributions in the United States

[2] Fletcher L. Byrom, Koppers Company, Inc., Pittsburgh, Pennsylvania, March 23, 1976.

to improper payments to public officials in this or other countries to influence purchases, tax concessions, or investment opportunities.

As a result there are an increasing number of voices from all directions calling for the promulgation of codes of conduct. Some demand government-issued decrees; others call for industry-wide codes; others for individual company codes.

As you all know, Koppers has a stated policy requiring compliance with all applicable laws anywhere. KOPPERS WILL OBEY THE LAW. I trust it is clear to everyone that the Koppers Company does not countenance illegal acts in any form and will punish appropriately anyone who commits such an act as a representative of the Company.

The question before us is not merely one of legal or illegal acts. Rather we are also concerned with the ethical and moral dimensions of actions which are not per se violations of the law. Many are attempting to describe specifically the actions of an employee which would be morally or ethically acceptable and those which are not.

I have been quoted as saying that I do not consider myself qualified to rewrite the Bible. Nor do I restrict this observation to Judeo-Christian teachings. All the great religions address themselves to the definition and desirability of moral and ethical conduct. I do not propose to attempt an improvement on those teachings.

As you all know the philosophy of management in this Company is one which places a premium on the quality of individual judgment. We do not issue voluminous procedure manuals, nor statements of limits of authority, nor complex organizational charts and manuals. It would be completely inconsistent with our style to attempt to replace individual judgment with specific instructions.

It is important, however, that we communicate a philosophy with regard to moral and ethical conduct in a way which will remove any feeling of ambiguity on your part as to what is expected of you.

I have frequently been asked how I can claim to be a Christian and a Chief Executive Officer at the same time. I have never found the two to be in contradiction. Economic measurements and compensation aimed at motivating good economic performance should not be understood to suggest any abandonment of moral principles in order to further the economic interests of the Company.

53

THE KOPPERS COMPANY DOES NOT EXPECT
ANYONE TO ACT IN ANY WAY CONTRARY TO HIS OR
HER HIGH MORAL AND ETHICAL STANDARDS
UNDER THE PRETEXT THAT IT WOULD BE IN THE
BEST INTEREST OF THE COMPANY.

Within each individual resides the will and the power to act
in good faith, to uphold laws written and unwritten, and to
understand the moral and ethical implications of our actions.
The conduct of business does not take place between inanimate
corporate entities but between individuals. We do not believe we
can create moral conscience through the issuance of a "code of
conduct" or by specific instructions for employee behavior.

Whet we can do and say, however, is that we accept the
teachings of the great religions in regard to moral and ethical
conduct.

We can and do say that we expect and pray that our
associates will be so guided.

We can and do say that we do not expect anyone to violate
such moral guidance under the belief that the Company would
benefit from acts that are contrary to individual conscience.

As a guide I might suggest that possibly the best test of
adherence to the dictates of conscience for a person with a family
might be to think whether you would be happy to tell your
spouse and children or other family members the details of the
actions you are contemplating.

If you would not want to do so, Koppers would not want
you to take the action.

Another test would be to decide whether you would be
willing to appear on television and explain your actions in detail.
Or whether you would be willing to explain your action to a
group of friends and neighbors.

In all of these cases if you would be unwilling to do so, we
would not want you to take the action under the assumption that
you would be helping Koppers.

The respected theologian, Paul Tillich, recently deceased,
said we must become comfortable with ambiguity in these times.
We do not want you to consider your personal conduct on behalf
of the Company to be a contradiction to your moral conscience.
It should not be and we ask that you not let it be.

My last point, then, is the only advice I will offer you: if you
are uncomfortable or have doubts as to what action to take, seek
advice from others for whom you have respect whether they be
peers, subordinates or superiors.

I trust that the above will help you to guide yourself, and hopefully will remove any misapprehensions with which you may have been struggling.

Twice Jesus gave the command:

A new commandment I give unto you, That ye love one another; as I have loved you, that ye also love one another. By this shall all men know that ye are my disciples, if ye have love one to another (John 13:34-35).

This message of Jesus about acting toward one another in love as the way to bring about the kingdom of heaven on earth is a simple lesson in theory but consistently neglected in practice. The Pittron story mentioned in the previous chapter is an example of its practice in the current world of industry.

Arnaud C. Marts, in his book *The Generosity of Americans,* points out that

the Christian Church was the conduit for the spiritual, intellectual and cultural elements of Western man.

High among these . . . values was the spirit and practice of private generosity for the public good, which the Christian Church called "charity," [that is,] "the act of loving all men as brothers because they are the sons of God."

Churches in America undertook their traditional practices of private generosity for the public good promptly, and for the next three centuries it was the Church which pioneered "nearly every educational and refining agency in the American culture."[3]

God in his infinite wisdom in creating us gave to us the freedom to choose—to choose to follow the leading of the Spirit of God and do good or to follow the evil spirit and to do wrong. This is a human characteristic not allied with any one group but all groups.

Why has the church been abandoning its traditional servant role in education, health, and even spiritual matters for what seems to be more and more the role of the critic?

[3] Arnaud C. Marts, *The Generosity of Americans* (Englewood Cliffs, N.J.: Prentice-Hall, Inc., 1966), pp. 20, 28, and 102.

If, as a businessman or educator, I'm not what I should be, then it must be asked, "Where has the church and its leadership been?" Most people in business are members of the church in their local communities. Many are active leaders of the church. Yet, in asking many of these people, I have yet to find one that has had a church leader come to the home or office to discuss whether Christian leadership is being given to the business or whether an attempt is being made to make decisions by Christian principles.

Instead, we in the churches are using our limited stock holdings in corporations and the public stockholders' meeting to be the critic, to attempt to legislate goodness in the hearts of people, and to proclaim our own "holiness."

Jesus' example was to condemn wrong wherever it occurred. It was also his example to sit down with sinners and publicans in their homes to influence them for good. He saw the potential for good in the unethical tax collector, Matthew.

He called him and changed him. He also said that the good shepherd would leave the ninety-nine sheep to seek and to save the one lost sheep.

The church leadership that says it is so choosy in the type of corporations in which it will invest and then gladly accepts the gift to the local church by the leader of that corporation therein establishes conflicting standards.

The church leadership readily condemns the motivation of corporation leadership and at the same time gladly accepts that leadership in United Way fund-raising efforts and a share of the funds therefrom to support many welfare institutions owned and operated by the church. Up to 85 percent of the support of many of these (Christian centers, neighborhood houses, YMCA and YWCA, Boys' Clubs, etc.) come from the United Way, which would be very ineffective without corporation support.

But church leadership says it does not have the funds to do

the things it once did. Again, the question is, Why? The early church exploded as a revolutionary force that changed Western civilization because it came at a time when people were tired of legalistic domination by the Roman and Jewish rulers, and people's hearts were hungry for spiritual inputs which the church through Christ's leadership provided. My observations suggest that people's hearts today are again hungering for spiritual inputs that the church should provide, but isn't.

Jesus condemned the act of sin without condemning the sinner. How different then is much of today's church leadership and its view of South Africa!

Business corporations are condemned for having investments in South Africa. Church leaders say, "Pull out." But who would be hurt most if such were done?—the black man whom we piously say we want to help.

On the one hand, we laity are urged to give to missions so that the hungry may be fed. Fill their stomachs that we may have an opportunity to give the people the gospel is the plea. However, pulling out of South Africa would empty stomachs. While I do not approve of the way blacks are often treated in South Africa, neither do I approve of the way we often treat one another in the U.S. But from personal observation, I know that the average black in South Africa is many times better off than the black anywhere else in Africa.

Being a good citizen within a country affords an opportunity to be a Christian witness and to give leadership that will change conditions in the direction of our example and Christ's teaching of loving one another. *You cannot be a servant-leader without being present.*

There are many other examples, including higher education, that could be cited where church leadership talks one way and acts another way. Our credibility gap is showing. Our facts are fuzzy because of inadequate research. Our strategy is poor because we are using the church and the name of Jesus Christ as a platform from which to attack those who are a part of us, and in the process we are chipping away at the platform whose collapse would eliminate the prospect of dealing with the real problems of enlistment into the kingdom of God and continued spiritual growth of the individual Christian. If wisdom comes from God, as the Bible teaches, then maybe the church needs to spend much more time in helping its individual members develop those characteristics of the image of God discussed in chapter 3.

To some, the above may seem like an unduly harsh critique of the church and a defense of the business corporation. It is not. It is an attempt to share a different perspective which I know from experience will work. I am a leader in the church and also an executive with a major corporation. Except for a relatively few church and/or business leaders, the same people are members of both institutions; so *why can't we get together* on common goals and strategies?

It Starts with You and Me

CHAPTER 7

I *am not ready* to give up on, abandon, or radically alter the form of the major institutions of our society. I *am ready and committed* to my own continued spiritual and intellectual growth and to any program that will help every individual truly to discover that the same God of creation made us all and gave us a responsibility to each other and for the rest of his creation and that a proper relationship to him is an essential first step in solving humanity's problems. Christ makes a difference in the life of a person; and the life of a servant Christian will make a positive difference in an institution, a community, or a nation.

The noted French traveler, philosopher, and government leader, de Tocqueville, observed, after traveling and studying in the United States of the nineteenth century, that when we see a need for a school, hospital, church, or other cultural service, a few local citizens form an association to meet the need, provide the leadership, and then support it. They do not expect the government to do so. Today, we in the church are more likely to point out the need and fault some person or institution for the existence of that need, rather than accept responsibility for doing something to meet the need ourselves. Few critics have either solved problems or motivated others to do so.

Freud has said that each love we experience, each loving act we perform, leaves a deposit—a result—on our own mind and personality. The critic also leaves a deposit that hardens and makes insensitive both the critic and the recipient of the criticism. We take away from the other person rather than give of ourselves.

Lowell had Jesus say in "The Vision of Sir Launfal":
"Who gives himself with his alms feeds three,
Himself, his hungering neighbor, and me."
I believe the time is ripe for the church to return fully to the servant-leader role. To do so requires a more complete understanding of Jesus Christ's role as the greatest servant, as well as the true meaning of leadership and how to achieve it. Again I return to quote Greenleaf on leadership:[1]

> One does not "learn" to be a leader the way one learns most things that are taught in college. Like anything else that is acquired, one will do better with a mentor or a coach than without one. . . . *Leadership overarches expertise,* and it cannot be reduced to a style. . . . Effective leadership defies categorization, but one is risked—four words: direction, values, competence (including judgment), and spirit.
>
> And if a flaw in the world is to be remedied, to the servant the process of change starts *in here,* in the servant, not *out there.* This is a difficult concept for that busybody, modern man.
>
> So it is with joy. Joy is inward, it is generated inside. It is not found outside and brought in. It is for those who accept the world as it is, part good, part bad, and who identify with the good by adding a little island of serenity to it.

The late Rabbi Abraham Joshua Heschel compared Judaism to "a messenger who forgot the message" and to "a well-guarded secret surrounded by an impenetrable wall." Perhaps he should have included Christianity and most other

[1] Taken from Robert K. Greenleaf, *The Servant as Leader* (Cambridge, Mass.: Center for Applied Studies, 1970, 1973). Copyright by Robert K. Greenleaf. Reproduced by permission.

religions. But it need not remain that way if we truly want to invite others inside the wall to share "the message."

YOU CAN MAKE A DIFFERENCE—I CAN MAKE A DIFFERENCE—EVERY PERSON CAN MAKE A DIFFERENCE. THE FACT IS—OUR ONLY CHOICE IS WHAT KIND OF DIFFERENCE WE MAKE—GOOD OR BAD. It is important, therefore, that the church and every Christian therein recognize that if the servant-leader role is to be played, we must do it. We can do it and make the world a better place in which to live, provided:

(1) The church returns to its commission of reaching people for Jesus Christ and teaching them that they may grow as servants. *Open the wall and share the message.*

(2) The church in its teaching ministry continually makes people aware of their capacity and potential as a result of being created in the image of God. *Open the wall and share the message.*

61

(3) The professional church leaders get more training in servant-leader qualities, either in the seminary or otherwise, in order that these qualities may be transferred to the laity who lead in the other institutions of society. *Open the wall and share the message.*

You can make a difference, and some are doing so now, by starting the process without waiting for someone else. More are needed—let's get going. The opportunity is great. The opportunity is now—there is no assurance of having it later.

BV   20266
4501.2
W564   Wheeley
1977   God can work through
        you

DEMCO